# YOUR KNOWLEDGE HAS VALUE

- We will publish your bachelor's and master's thesis, essays and papers

- Your own eBook and book - sold worldwide in all relevant shops

- Earn money with each sale

## Upload your text at www.GRIN.com and publish for free

**Bibliographic information published by the German National Library:**

The German National Library lists this publication in the National Bibliography;
detailed bibliographic data are available on the Internet at http://dnb.dnb.de .

**Imprint:**

Copyright © 2015 GRIN Verlag
Print and binding: Books on Demand GmbH, Norderstedt Germany
ISBN: 9783668008342

**This book at GRIN:**

https://www.grin.com/document/302077

**Lore Li**

# Shakespeare's Authorship Question. A Short Input to a Long Discussion

GRIN Verlag

**GRIN - Your knowledge has value**

Since its foundation in 1998, GRIN has specialized in publishing academic texts by students, college teachers and other academics as e-book and printed book. The website www.grin.com is an ideal platform for presenting term papers, final papers, scientific essays, dissertations and specialist books.

**Visit us on the internet:**

http://www.grin.com/

http://www.facebook.com/grincom

http://www.twitter.com/grin_com

FREIE SCHULE ZINNOWITZ

# Shakespeare's authorship question

A short input to a long discussion

# Content

# 1 Introduction

William Shakespeare was born in 1564 and died in 1616 in Stratford-upon-Avon farther writing plays like *Romeo and Juliet, Othello, Macbeth, A Midsummer Night's Dream* and others. He was a brilliant playwright creating nearly 40 productions and 154 sonnets, while dwelling in London. This is at least the majority opinion taught in schools.

There is however reason for doubt. While dealing a bit deeper with Shakespeare you unavoidably will come to the point that opinions differ in the question if he truly was who he pretended to be. Imagine the magnificent bard was not the author of all the dramas, comedies, history plays and poems. Or could it be possible that this famous name was just a pseudonym? And if it was, then the question is why? Which clues for and against are existing?

In the English lessons we learned the prevailing aspects along with the common view about the grand composer and his plays. After a rough contribution into the authorship debate more questions emerged and the foundation of this term paper was laid.

To come to one of many answers, this work will be structured at first in a short biography of Shakespeare and an overview of his time concerning the theatre and authorship in general. Afterwards I would like to explore positions that assume Shakespeare not to be the man who is thought to be the drafter Shakespeare. On the other hand also the opposing view will be presented and explained. To forge an own profound opinion it is significant to have a review about this complex of themes.

A detailed presentation of my own view regarding arguments for and against Shakespeare from Stratford as the writer will be followed by a final synopsis and prospect of the issue. So the focus in this work is more on investigate the Stratford-man than on other theories, even though these will come up for discussion. Because of their multifacetedness it would go beyond the scopes of this term paper.

# 2 Overviews of Shakespeare and his time

## 2.1 Short biography of Shakespeare

When now writing about William Shakespeare the person from Stratford-upon-Avon (Warwickshire, England) is meant, who is the bard Shakespeare according to the most common opinion. That implies this biography is written as this man would be the author.

Shakespeare's exact date of birth is unknown, but his baptism on the 26th of April 1564 is certified by a church record[1]. He was born as the third child to John Shakespeare, a successful leather merchant and alderman, and Mary Arden, whose father was a landowning farmer. There is no evidence that he attended school, but it is assumed that he acquired education in the King's New School in Stratford.

When he was 18 years old he married the eight years older Anne Hathaway on the 28th November 1582 and their first daughter Susanna was born after six months. 1585 Anne gave birth to the twins Hamnet and Judith, the boy died at the age of 11[2]. The next seven years until 1592 are called the "lost years" because it is a period without existing records about Shakespeare or his actions. But there are certain speculations that range from starting his theatrical career in London[3], being a country schoolmaster to fleeing from the landlord Thomas Lucy because of illegal deer hunting. In the late 1580s he probably moved to London because 1592 some of Williams plays were performed in London and Robert Greene, a London playwright, attacked him in the Stationers' Register[4] by writing: "There is an upstart Crow, beautified with our feathers, that with his Tiger's heart wrapped in a Player's hide, supposes he is as well able to bombast out a blank verse as the best of you: and being an absolute Johannes factotum, is in his own conceit the only Shake-scene in a country[5]."

His first plays were the trilogy *Henry VI* probably in 1589-91, then other performances ensued like *The Comedy of Errors* (presumably 1592) and his poem *Venus and Adonis* was released in 1593.

He became a part owner of 'The Globe'[6], which opened in 1599[7] and 'The Blackfriars' theatre and actor and member of the theatrical company 'Lord Chamberlain's Men' in 1594.

---

[1] Laura Grimm, Leanne French, Eudie Pak (2015)
[2] Ibid. *Shakespeare Biography* http://shakespeare.about.com/od/shakespeareslife/a/Biography.htm (08.04.2015)
[3] Poemhunter.com (2015)
[4] A guild publication (cf. http://www.biography.com/people/william-shakespeare-9480323#synopsis) (16.03.2015)
[5] Bastian Conrad correlates the „Shake-scene" not with Shakespeare but with Edward Alleyn, a famous actor. (cf. Bastian Conrad 2014, p.88 f.)
[6] 'The Globe' was a London theatre at the south bank of the river themsis.

The same year, the tragedy *Romeo and Juliet* was drafted[8] and by 1597 he possessed the largest house in Stratford. The comedy *Much Ado About Nothing* was written one year afterwards.

His spectacle troupe was famous in such a way that it was patronized by King James I. since 1603 to 1625 and hence they changed their name to 'The King's Men'. After 1600 Shakespeare wrote the so-called later works, almost all tragedies such as *Hamlet*, probably referring to his dead son. 1605 *Macbeth* was acted out at the Globe Theatre and the last play possibly was a collaboration with John Fletcher (*Two Noble Kinsmen* 1613)

After 1610 he went back to Stratford-upon-Avon and died there on the 23rd April 1616.

In total he wrote[9] about 37 plays[10], other sources claim 38[11] depending on the conumeration of the collaborative work with John Fletcher or even 40 works when including the two lost plays *Love's Labour's Won* and *Cardenio*[12]. Additionally 154 sonnets and five poems are attributed to this writer.

## 2.2 Theatre and authorship in the Elizabethan and Jacobean time

The Elizabethan era started with the coronation of Queen Elizabeth I. in 1558 and lasted until her death in 1603. This time is also called the 'Golden Age' because the Queen settled the conflict between the Catholics and Protestants. During her reign the first theatres were built in London. Previously the establishing acting troupes performed in inn-yards or taverns[13]. Around 1576 James Burbage constructed 'The Theatre', which was used by the Lord Chamberlain's Men from 1594-96. Several open air amphitheatres like 'The Rose' or 'The Curtain' opened and were mainly used in the summer months. The playhouses had a capacity of approximately 1500-3000 people and the cheapest standing places in the groundlings were priced at one penny. With paying more, like the nobles, the seats in the galleries were more comfortable, covered and had even a better view on the event.

Throughout the time of the plagues 1593 and 1603 all theatres in London were closed and from 1596-97 they were banned from the city because of the high risk of infection combined with the authorities' fear of tumults and riots.

---

[7] Laura Grimm, Leanne French, Eudie Pak (2015)
[8] Lee Jamieson (n.d.) *Shakespeare Timeline*
[9] List of Shakespeare's plays see enclosure app. 1
[10] Laura Grimm, Leanne French, Eudie Pak (2015)
[11] Lee Jamieson (n.d.) *List of Shakespeare* http://shakespeare.about.com/od/theplays/a/ List_of_Shakespeare_Plays.htm (04.04.2015)
[12] Amanda Mabillard (2014) *How Many Plays Did Shakespeare Write?* http://www.shakespeare-online.com/plays/numberofplays.html (04.04.2015)
[13] Linda Alchin (2015) *Elizabethan Theater, Playhouses & Inn-Yards*

The Queen herself watched performances in her own residence, with specially engaged spectacle troupes[14] and encouraged the theatrical growth.

The mentality in England at that time was more liberal than in the other European countries. Therefore there were more and better possibilities to get creative in writing or acting. Yet it was not allowed to pen against the church or the Queen.

King James I. was crowned in 1603. He was very interested in the arts, the theatre and its plays, and especially in drama. He became the patron of the Lord Chamberlain's Men very shortly after his inauguration.

Actors were held in low esteem, but the reputation increased towards the end of the 16th century[15]. Nevertheless they needed the patronage of a noble, not to rate as vagabond and be punished as one. The social conventions determined that aristocrats were not allowed to write any plays or literature of such kind. That is why they often used pseudonyms when publishing something written.

# 3  Theories about his authorship

The first doubts[16] about the true identity of the man who composed all the writings, were risen roughly 150 years after William Shakespeare's death, when Herbert Lawrence wrote a book about the possibility that Shakespeare was only a pseudonym in 1769. 1780 James Wilmot wanted to draft a biography about the man from Stratford, but could not find any book about Shakespeare or other evidence that sustained him as the author. Therefore Wilmot supposed another candidate, **Sir Francis Bacon**, to be the composer. Delia Bacon represented the same idea in her book *The Philosophy of the Plays of Shakespeare Unfolded,* 1857. Likewise Mark Twain came to the same point with his book *Is Shakespeare dead?* inspired by George Greenwood. Several theories were developed, essays, books and articles were written about **Christopher Marlowe** as the real Shakespeare (Wilbur Ziegler: *It was Marlowe* 1895, Calvin Hoffman: *The Murder of the Man Who Was "Shakespeare"* 1955) or **Edward de Vere, 17th Earl of Oxford** (J. Thomas Looney: *"Shakespeare" Identified in Edward De Vere, the Seventeenth Earl of Oxford* 1920, Charlton Ogburn: *The Mysterious William Shakespeare* 1984) or **Ben Jonson** (Joseph C. Hart: *The Romance of Yachting* 1848) or **Sir Edward Dyer** (Alden Brooks: *Will Shakespeare and the Dyer's Hand* 1943). Furthermore various films exist today about the authorship and there is a lot of debate about the subject.

---

[14] Prof. Dr. Theo Stemmler (2012)
[15] Ibid.
[16] The Shakespeare Authorship Roundtable (n.d.)

Added together there are approximately 60 candidates that are presumed to be the true "Bard of Avon". The following sub items will approach some selected theories as well as the conviction that Shakespeare wrote Shakespeare.

## 3.1 Christopher Marlowe

First of all, this theory strictly makes a distinction between the author Shakespeare and the (business)man from Stratford-upon-Avon most time written as "Shakspere" (or Shexpere, Shackspere, Shaxper,...[17]) with a phonetically short first syllable. Even if the orthography, spelling and grammar in general was not fixed at this time, it has to be noticed that the names were written how it was pronounced[18]. So Shak- and Shakespeare are most probably different names/ names of different persons.

This confidence is based on the assumption that Christopher Marlowe used the name Shakespeare as a pseudonym because he got into dire straits when writing against the church. Marlowe feigned his death in 1593 and engaged William Shakespeare to be his "face" in public.

Also it is explained that the artistic pursuit of Shakespeare would have begun too late. The life expectancy in the 16th/17th century was short with around 40 years, but he started his literary activity at the age of 26 and moreover there was no parallel activity of Shakespeare and Marlowe even though both were born in the same year. That also would mean that Shakespeare never had a development and training in writing before his first opus *Venus and Adonis*. Marlowe already had worked as a dramatist and as a translator when he was 30 years old. [19]

## 3.2 Edward de Vere, 17th Earl of Oxford

Proponents, who believe in Edward de Vere, the 17th Earl of Oxford as the true composer of all Shakespearean works are called "Oxfordians". It is the most popular alternative after the leading theory and dominating opinion that Shakespeare was the author.

The nobleman Edward de Vere who lived from 1550 – 1604 was a known playwright and poet[20]. In the position as the Lord Great Chamberlain, he was renowned at court of Queen Elizabeth, who determined a subvention in the amount of £1000 yearly to him from 1568 until her death. His authorship is presumed behind the nom de plume Shakespeare because he had

---

[17] William Henry Burr (1886)
[18] Bastian Conrad (2014) p.76
[19] Ibid. p.43-44
[20] Neue Shake-speare Gesellschaft (2013)

very close connections to the court and its life, which is thematized in plenty of Shakespeare's plays.

Furthermore this high regarded man had a prime education firstly private and then at Cambridge University and Gray's Inn[21] where he acquired knowledge of the law, dancing, cosmography, music, several languages like Latin, Greek and French. During a Grand Tour through Europe he made many new experiences and deepened for instance his understanding of other nations and their cultures.

The argument that de Vere died too early in order to have been Shakespeare is here refuted by saying that the works might have been published later than penned[22].

## 3.3 Francis Bacon

The so-called "Baconians" believe in Sir Francis Bacon[23] who lived from 1561 – 1626 as the producer of the Shakespearean plays. The Viscount St. Alban had an excellent education, at first privately, later at the Cambridge University and at the Gray's Inn. He travelled extensively through the European courts (he spent e.g. from 1576-79 with the French Court) and was member in various circles, for example the Elizabethan intelligence network.

Moreover he wrote speeches for pageants at the court and stage plays in diverse styles and it is stated that he was able to imitate other people's way of writing.

It is said that he had a relish and preference to theatre and poetry and the Shakespearean oeuvre would match to his experiences, interests and mind-set. Also fellow men like Ben Jonson characterised him as the "mark and acme" of the English language and friends pictured him as a "concealed poet".

## 3.4 William Stanley, 6th Earl of Derby

Another candidate is William Stanley, living from 1561 – 1642. The "Derbyites" view him, the son-in-law of Edward de Vere, as the real author, in virtue of his education at St. John's College in Oxford, his study at Gray's Inn, his extended travels in Europe beginning in 1582 and his own player troupe 'The Derby's Men'. Later, in 1594 he inherited the earldom from his late older brother (Ferdinando Stanley, 5th Earl of Derby).

---

[21] „Gray's Inn is one of the four Inns of Court which have the exclusive right to call men and women to the Bar of England and Wales. The Inn exists to support, educate and develop its student barrister members [...]." Retrieved from: https://www.graysinn.org.uk/the-inn (10.04.2015)

[22] The De Vere Society (n.d.)

[23] The Shakespearean Authorship Trust (Julia Cleave, Kevin Gilvary, William Leahy,...) (n.d.) *Sir Francis Bacon*

A literary activity is given through the fact that George Fenner, a spy, who expounded in June 1599 that the Earl was "busied only in penning comedies for the common players."[24]

The equal first name William and the same initials W. S. from Stanley and Shakespeare are strong indications for proponents of this thesis to assume that Shakespeare was the pseudonym of the Earl.[25]

## 3.5  Group theory

This speculation is based on the not uncommon collaborations of authors in those days. For example Edward de Vere, Francis Bacon, Mary Sidney Herbert, Roger Manners and many more[26] have been suggested to be members of the writing team behind the penname Shakespeare. But the number and the names of all persons are shifting and not clearly defined.

The idea is suggested because it seems to be impossible for one person to acquire the huge variety of everything that is written in the entire oeuvre[27].

## 3.6  William Shak(e)spe(a)re

On the other hand there is the opinion that William Shakespeare from Stratford was the popular author. The supporters of this theory are called "Stratfordians" and they do not differ between the variant spelling Shakespeare or Shakespeare like adherents of other positions do.

They weaken the argument pertaining to his insufficient school education with a safe assumption that he attended a very good Grammar school in Stratford, where he learned to speak Latin fluently and acquired the Classics. Furthermore he did not need to attend university because his home town was "a melting pot of intellectual modernity, enriched with immigrants from all over the continent"[28] and it is referred to autodidacts like Thomas Mann. In addition to this, it is demented that it was an unprofessional conduct for aristocrats to write dramas for the theatre.

---

[24] Shakespeare Authorship Roundtable *William Stanley, Earl of Derby* Retrieved from: http://www.shakespeareauthorship.org/authors/stanley.html (07.04.2015)
[25] John Raithel (n.d.)
[26] The Shakespearean Authorship Trust *Group Theory of Authorship* Retrieved from: http://www.shakespeareanauthorshiptrust.org.uk/pages/candidates/collab.htm (04.04.2015)
[27] Shakespeare Authorship Roundtable *Group Theory, Literary Collaboration*
[28] Hans-Dieter Gelfert (2014), p.16

# 4 Own argumentation

## 4.1 Contra Shakespeare

The main arguments against Shak(e)spe(a)re as Shakespeare are in every "Anti-Stratfordian" theory the same, like Robert Brazil expounded in his essay *The Shakespeare Problem* (2007).

Firstly the only written words of Shakespeare from Stratford are merely six shaky signatures, that impossibly can come from a man who had to have written hundreds of text pages, thus more testifies his nearly illiteracy. This should also be shown by his parents' and daughter Judith's missing ability to write, what is cognizable in their using of marks instead of a name or signature. But suppose he was such a genius, it would have been feasible that his children were not well educated when he did not see the necessity to do this.

In addition to that, in his testament there is no paper, book, manuscript or any other written document found. And if he did not bequeath suchlike, it is even more unlikely that he possessed books let alone a library. But then the question rises where he got all the knowledge from that is within the whole lecture attributed to Shakespeare.

Beyond that, the records and evidences for his schooling are not findable and proponents only "think he may have been educated in the King's School in Stratford because that would have been typical for a child with a father who is an alderman."[29]

And because there is nothing that proves his matriculation at any university or higher academy, it seems impossible to learn all the cultures and languages like Latin, Italian, French, Dutch, Spanish, and Greek above the classical literature, enormous knowledge about judiciary, philosophy, history, military, arts, mathematics, seafaring, courtly amusements as tennis, equestrian sport and courtly etiquette and politics[30] autodidactical and self-taught.

Especially the courtly aspects in the poems and plays of Shakespeare are indicative of a better educated candidate like Edward de Vere, Francis Bacon, Christopher Marlowe or William Stanley who all had connections to the royals or several other high rated personalities, an excellent schooling and had done a lot of voyages. The writer had known the high society of England very well, so he required close ties and relations to it, what cannot be substantiated for Shakespeare.

Another argument against Shakespeare as composer is that there aren't any documents found which prove his authorial or artistical activity[31]. Neither have diaries, manuscripts, letters nor

---

[29] Albert Joss Paulsen (2014, October 17) said by Rebecca Lemon.
[30] Bastian Conrad (2014) p.45
[31] Ibid. p.37

9

reports of his friends been detected. As well there is nothing in the chronicles of Stratford-upon-Avon that hold him to have been an author.

His years in London (1592-1612) are similarly not documented, in terms of someone who encountered a poet named William Shakespeare, but an owner of properties, businessman, merchant, shareholder of theatres and some more. As an actor, for example in 1598 in Ben Jonson's *Every man in his Humour*[32] or *Sejanus* (1603) shown in the cast lists, only a Will Shakespeare is mentioned. However Shakespeare has to be meant, since who else should have been this actor instead? - Either a completely different person or him – both possibilities are there.

Generally the question rises why Shakespeare should have differed between a family and a bard name[33]. Almost every formal document like baptism, marriage, lawsuits, death and testament has the name with a phonetically short first syllable (Shaksper [as inhabitant of Southwark 1596] or Shexpere, Shackspeare, Schackspeare [as plaintiff in a suit 1604, 1609, 1612]) and nearly on every printed work the name "Shakespeare" has emerged, with being hyphenated in "Shake" and "speare" about half of all the times[34]. This separation within the name through a hyphen should be an indication for a pseudonym[35].

When the man from Stratford died, in 1616, no eulogies were published. Even so it was common at this time that laudations or encomiums were written to a deceased poet by other writers. There are some contemporary poets whose death had not been mentioned by somebody else, but why was the prominent bard Shakespeare appreciated primarily in the eulogy in the "First Folio", seven years after his death? At this, the dedication by Ben Johnson is only drafted to "The Author Mr. William Shakespeare" not to a Shakspere (Shexpere, Shackspeare, etc.). The first page of the First Folio captioned with "To the Reader" advices "Looke not on his Picture, but his Booke"[36] what can be seen as an indication for Shakespeare as pseudonym because when the picture is showing Shakspere, the dummy, the eyes should not be focussed on this man, but on the writings in the book of the real author.

Moreover there is the question, why Shakspere had not published all of his works during his life when he wrote as a job and for money[37]. But when looking at another chronology of his

---

[32] Robert Brazil (2007)
[33] Complete list with various spellings of his name in reference to the particular case in William Henry Burr's *Bacon and Shakspere* (1886)
[34] Bastian Conrad (2014)
[35] Robert Detobel and Uwe Laugwitz (1997) p.15
[36] The whole „First Folio": http://internetshakespeare.uvic.ca/Library/facsimile/book/SLNSW_F1/2/?zoom=506
[37] Robert Brazil (2007)

plays[38], it is obvious that all of them were performed or produced within his lifetime, merely a lot of them (36 performances) were printed firstly in 1623 in the First Folio.

When the *Shakespeare's Sonnets* were printed in 1609 Shakespeare had not done anything against the dissemination of the poems, comprising a very intimate content. Furthermore the publisher Thomas Thorpe wrote in the dedication of the sonnets "by.our.ever.living.poet"[39] that point to the fact that the author was already dead (Edward de Vere) or known as dead (Christopher Marlowe). And it is said that the sonnets are not having parallels or bearing reference to Shakespeare's life[40].

The "lost years" of Shakespeare are proposing a conundrum. Nothing documenting his actions in those years from 1585 - 1593 exists or has been found. Suppose he had literary training or socialised with the high society at the court or travelled through the European courts, all together, it seems a bit more plausible to assume him as the author. But taking just the fact that there is nothing recorded, the speculations are giving the impression of compulsive attempts to explain Shakespeare being appropriate.

The Shakespeare Monument in Stratford was made around 1623 showing a man who holds a sack of grain what most likely valuates him as a successful tradesman. Not until the restoration in 1749 he was shown with a quill demonstrating him as a playwright.

Edward Alleyn, who was a famous actor and also theatre owner in that time, enumerated all contemporary dramatists, actors or people otherwise connected with the theatre and left Shakespeare out. In the same way Phillip Henslowe, owner of the theatre "The Rose", never mentioned Shakespeare or Shakespeare in his detailed diary accounts about payments, productions, purchases etc. neither to be a writer nor an actor[41]. Not even Shakespeare's son-in-law Dr. John Hall, husband of his daughter Susanna, had known his own father-in-law as dramatist or the like.

## 4.2 Pro Shakespeare

Scholars who believe in Shak(e)spe(a)re from Stratford-upon-Avon as the true composer, propose the possibility that the different way of writing his name is caused by the flexible spelling and grammar structures in the Elizabethan time[42]. But they are disregarding the fact

---

[38] See enclosure app. 1
[39] OxquarryBooks Ltd. (2014) is showing the dedication.
[40] Bastian Conrad (2014) p.73
[41] David B. Schajer (2013) http://shakespearesolved.blogspot.de/2013/01/shakespeare-and-philip-henslowe.html
[42] Alex Knapp (2011)

that the different spellings can be linked with the distinction between private life in his home town and the "business name" as an author.

The argument that it was not conform the social norms to be an aristocratic playwright they deny by saying that the English nobility was relatively free to write. Like Sir Fulke Greville did (*Alaham* ca. 1600, *Mustapha* 1603-1608) or dramatist Sir Francis Beaumont who wrote many plays in cooperation with John Fletcher for The King's Men[43]. This is an issue which I cannot evaluate whether it is wrong or correct because there is no airtight prove that this is true. But if it is true, that would not mean that all noblemen based theories would automatically collapse like a house of cards for the valid argument of the education and better knowledge of them still stands.

Another main reason for the Stratford-man should be that in his town there was a Grammar school. Presuming he attended this institution of education, it sounds reasonable to agree that he gained a solid basic training. Other sources claim in fact: "Education was different then. Grammar school provided a rich literary training: grammar, composition, rhetoric, poetry, figurative language, the classics. [...] And the Stratford grammar school was good."[44] It also seems to be coherent to me that he had gone to school, precisely because his father was an alderman and not poor.

Notwithstanding the fact that there are no evidences of travels or further training in any way. So the inquiry where he got the huge knowledge still continues. For it is known that travel broadens the mind and is significant to gather experiences, especially all those which are applied in the numerous works of Shakespeare. Normally there has to be something of this kind. Though according to proponents is was not necessary because his hometown was called the "third university of England" and it had immigrants from several European countries[45] with the result that an easy exchange of cultural identities, languages and styles was possible.

The Collaborations of William Shakespeare should be a lead against a titled author who had never been in contact with a common composer[46]. That certainly disagrees with, for instance, the proven collaboration of Francis Beaumont and John Fletcher. But the question remains how it was possible to prevent the collaborators from talking? With money?

---

[43] Hildegard Hammerschmidt-Hummel (2001) p.274
[44] Prof. Peter Saccio (2013)
[45] Hans-Dieter Gelfert (2014) p.16
[46] Alex Knapp (2011)

Then it is cited as a reason that the author wrote his works with certain theatres and actors in mind so he had to know them optimally[47], nevertheless also the high society had free entrance to the playhouses.

In the First Folio, Ben Jonson relates the writer posthumously to the Shakespeare Monument in Stratford-upon-Avon, evidently he had no doubt about the authorship[48].

## 4.3  Summary

To summarize my own investigation, I found more conclusive points against the majority's opinion to see Shak(e)spe(a)re as the composer and brilliant playwright William Shakespeare. So I would call myself an "Anti-Stratfordian" and I would support and agree with the theory of Christopher Marlowe being the author because his thesis endures also when it is not true that the aristocratic writing was not standardized, since it is based on Marlowe's escape from execution. Some other poets had already been imprisoned or executed (John Greenwood, Henry Barrowe) because of "seditious" books or scriptures in April 1593 and Marlowe appeared as summoned to the crown council (1593, May 20). An alleged killing in a dispute about a bill payment followed (30th May), the corpse could have been the previous day executed John Penry[49] to make the public believe in this reputed elimination of a "dissenter".

After hiring Shakespeare from Stratford, who probably was in London 1593, Marlowe could continue to write, now under pseudonym.

Moreover he graduated at the Corpus Christi College, Cambridge (as Master of Arte) and is supposed to have travelled through Europe from May 1572 – June 1575 with Philip Sidney and wrote such as *The Tragedie of Dido, Queen of Carthage* first printed 1594, *Tamburlaine part I and II* 1590, *Doctor Faustus* 1604, *Hero and Leander* 1598, *The Jew of Malta* 1833[50] and further translations. Besides that he had proven connections to many noble and high rated persons (for instance William and Robert Cecil, Henry Wriothesley, Michael Drayton, Ferdinando Stanley)[51].

Although interpreting the text under Shakespeare's Monument as hidden message[52] seems too far-fetched to me.

---

[47] Ibid.
[48] Bastian Conrad sees ambiguities in the dedication, especially in the preamble having seventeen lines. (cf. Bastian Conrad 2014, p.79 f.)
[49] Bastian Conrad (2014) p.128 ff.
[50] The Marlowe Society (2015)
[51] Ibid. p.168
[52] Ibid. p.176

According to stylistic comparing investigations the length of used words is characteristic for every author. When T. C. Mendenhall compared Marlowe's and Shakespeare's compositions (1887) he found out that both curves are nearly identical. Peter Farey did word- and style analysis and came to the conclusion that the statistical correspondence from Marlowe and Shakespeare was higher than between sundry contemporary poets, whereas there are opponents declaring both to be similar in linguistic ability, but Marlowe never had a streak of humour or female figures in his works while Shakespeare did have.

In spite of it all, to me Christopher Marlowe seems to represent a serious candidate to be the author behind (the pseudonym) William Shakespeare.

## 5 Conclusion and prospect

This ongoing debate about the authorship of Shakespeare's plays remains unsolved.

There are indications and clues letting one presume that Shak(e)spe(a)re was not the true drafter of the works attributed to him, but I have a notion that watertight evidences never will be found, for who registers an "employment" as front-man?

It is a matter of believe or conviction determined by good arguments.

During my investigation of this contestation, my persuasion concerning what I learned about Shakespeare in school, changed. Now I think, there should be a deeper step into this theme in literature lessons due the fact that there are other serious theories beside the major view, probably coming through never being introduced to these. Pupils and students should forge an own opinion. And, what is more, this whole topic teaches the lesson that you should not blindly believe anything that is taught at school without checking it yourself.

# 6 Sources

## 6.1 Electronic Resources

Alchin, L. (2015). *Elizabethan Theatre History Timeline*. Retrieved from:
http://www.elizabethan-era.org.uk (19.03.2015).

Alchin, L. (2015). *Elizabethan Theater, Playhouses & Inn-Yards*. Retrieved from:
http://www.william-shakespeare.info/william-shakespeare-biography-elizabethan-theatre-playhouse-inn-yards.htm (19.03.2015).

Ancestry.com. (2004). *Looking for Shakespeare. The origins of the authorship question*. Retrieved from:
http://freepages.genealogy.rootsweb.ancestry.com/~shakespeare/poet/authorship.htm (18.03.2015).

Burr, W. H. (1886). *Bacon and Shakspere*. (Released March 12, 2012). Retrieved from:
http://www.gutenberg.org/files/39121/39121-h/39121-h.htm (07.04.2015).

Brazil, R. (2007). *The Shakespeare Problem*. Retrieved from:
http://www.elizabethanauthors.org/problem.htm (19.03.2015).

Brown, H. (2014). *Shakespeare's patrons & other essays*. Retrieved from:
http://www.shakespeare-online.com/biography/patronjames.html (19.03.2015).

Cleave, J., Gilvary, K., Leahy, W., Rylance, M., Wilson, L. (n.d.) *The Shakespearean Authorship Trust. Who really wrote Shakespeare's plays?* Retrieved from:
http://www.shakespeareanauthorshiptrust.org.uk (03.04.2015).

Detobel, R., Laugwitz, U. (1997). *Neues Shake-speare Journal. Band 1. Zum Stand der Diskussion*. Retrieved from: http://www.laugwitz.de/shakespeare/JB1_A5.pdf (08.04.2015).

Grimm, L., French, L., Pak, E. (2015). *William Shakespeare Biography*. Retrieved from:
http://www.biography.com/people/william- shakespeare-9480323#synopsis (16.03.2015).

Hagl, S. (2015). *Der rätselhafte Dramatiker*. Retrieved from: http://www.gral.de/gralswelt/gralswelt_archiv/gralswelt_812014/der_raetselhafte_dramatiker (19.03.2015).

Internet Shakespeare Editions. (2011). *Facsimile Viewer: First Folio (New South Wales)*. Retrieved from: http://internetshakespeare.uvic.ca/Library/facsimile/book/SLNSW_F1/1/?zoom=506 (09.04.2015).

Jamieson, L. (n.d.). Shakespeare Timeline. Retrieved from:
http://shakespeare.about.com/od/shakespeareslife/a/Shakespeare_Timeline.htm (16.03.2015).

Knapp, A. (2011). *Forbes. Yes, Shakespeare Really Did Write Shakespeare.* Retrieved from:
http://www.forbes.com/sites/alexknapp/2011/10/19/yes-shakespeare-really-did-write-shakespeare/ (09.04.2015).

Mabillard, A. (2014). *Shakespeare Q & A: The King's Men.* Retrieved from:
http://shakespeare-online.com/faq/kingsmen.html (19.03.2015).

Neue Shake-speare Gesellschaft. (2013). *Shake-speare. A short life of Edward de Vere, 17th
Earl of Oxford.* Retrieved from: http://www.shakespeare-today.de/front_content.php?idart=108 (04.04.2015).

Oxquarry Books Ltd. (2014). *Shakespeare's Sonnets. The Dedication.* Retrieved from:
http://www.shakespeares-sonnets.com/dedication (09.04.2015).

Paulsen, A. J. (2014, October 17) *William Shakespeare: The Conspiracy Theories* [Video
file]. Retrieved from: https://www.youtube.com/watch?v=mFvKHX9jY9U&index=
1&list=PLcNcNGxtV-Jix7lkpWoJ6aFxiX_XDfy1W (07.04.2015).

PBS.org. (2005). *The Merchant of Venice. Who was Shakespeare?.* Retrieved from:
http://www.pbs.org/wgbh/masterpiece/merchant/shakespeare.html (18.03.2015).

Poemhunter.com. (2015). *William Shakespeare. Biography of William Shakespeare.*
Retrieved from: http://www.poemhunter.com/william-shakespeare/biography/
(16.03.2015).

Raithel, J. (n.d.). *The URL of Derby. The Contenders.* Retrieved from:
http://www.rahul.net/raithel/Derby/contenders.html?27,35 (07.04.2015).

Saccio, P. (2013, October 24). *Prof. Peter Saccio destroys the Shakespeare authorship
question* [Video file]. Retrieved from:
https://www.youtube.com/watch?v=D2YHLjE1Wh4 (09.04.2015).

Schajer, D.B. (2013). *Shakespeare Solved. Shakespeare and Philip Henslowe.* Retrieved
from: http://shakespearesolved.blogspot.de/2013/01/shakespeare-and-philip-henslowe.html (09.04.2015).

Shakespeare Authorship Roundtable. (n.d.). *History of the Controversy. Significant Dates.*
Retrieved from: http://www.shakespeareauthorship.org/controversy/history.html
(19.03.2015).

Stemmler, T. (2012). *Elisabethanisches Theater: Eine Bühne für alle Stände.* Retrieved from:
http://universal_lexikon.deacademic.com/233478/elisabethanisches_Theater%3A_Ein
e_B%C3%BChne_f%C3%BCr_alle_St%C3%A4nde (19.03.2015).

The De Vere Society. (n.d.). *Dating Shakespeare's Plays: A Critical Review of the Evidence.*
    Retrieved from: http://www.deveresociety.co.uk/index.php?page=datingProject
    (11.04.2015).

The Marlowe Society. (2015). *Christopher Marlowe's Work. Published Works.* Retrieved
    from: http://www.marlowe-society.org/marlowe/work/work.html#FootNoteP
    (09.04.2015).

## 6.2 Books

Conrad, Bastian. (2014). *Der wahre Shakespeare: Christopher Marlowe. Zur Lösung des
    Jahrhunderte alten Autorschaftsproblems.* (2., revised and expanded edition). Munich:
    Buch&media GmbH.

Gelfert, Hans-Dieter. (2014). *William Shakespeare in seiner Zeit.* Munich: C.H.Beck oHG.

Hammerschmidt-Hummel, H. (2001). *Die verborgene Existenz des William Shakespeare.
    Dichter und Rebell im katholischen Untergrund.* Freiburg: Herder.

# 7 Enclosure

*App. 1:*

## Chronology of plays attributed to Shakespeare[53]

1592 March 3, *Henry VI Part I* is produced. First printed 1594

1592-93 *Henry VI, Part II* first performed. First print 1594

1592-93 *Henry VI, Part III* first performed. First printed 1623

1594 January 24 *Titus Andronic*us first performance. First print 1594

1594 December 28, Confirmed performance of *The Comedy of Errors*. First printed 1623

1593-94 *Taming of the Shrew* first performed. First print 1623

1594-95 *Two Gentlemen of Verona* first performance. First printed 1623

1594-95 *Love's Labour's Lost* first performed. First print 1598

1594-95 *Romeo and Juliet* first performance. First printed 1597

1595-96 *A Midsummer Night's Dream* first performed. First print 1600

1596-97 *The Merchant of Venice* first performed. First printed 1600

1597-98 *Henry IV, Part I* first performed. First print 1598

1597-98 *Henry IV, Part II* first performance. First printed 1600

1598-99 *Much Ado About Nothing* first performed. First print 1600

1598-99 *Henry V* first performed. First printed 1600

1599-00 *As You Like It* first performed. First print 1623

1600-01 *Julius Caesar* first performance. First printed 1623

1601 February 7 First Recorded production of *Richard II*. First printed 1597

1600-01 *Richard III* first Recorded performance. First print 1597

1600-01 *Hamlet* first performed. First printed 1603

1600-01 *The Merry Wives of Windsor* first performance. First print 1602

1602 February 2 First Recorded production of *Twelfth Night*. First printed 1623

1602-03 *All's Well That Ends Well* first performed. First print 1623

1604 February 7 First Recorded production of *Troilus and Cressida*. First printed 1609

1604 December 26 First performance of *Measure for Measure*. First print 1623

1604-05 *Othello* first performed. First printed 1622

1606 December 26 First recorded performance of *King Lear*. First print 1608

---

[53] Linda Alchin (2014) http://www.william-shakespeare.info/william-shakespeare-play-chronology-dates.htm (04.04.2015).

1605-06 *Macbeth* first performance. First printed 1623

1606-07 *Antony and Cleopatra* first performed. First print 1623

1607-08 *Coriolanus* first performed. First printed 1623

1607-08 *Timon of Athens* first performance. First print 1623

1608-09 *Pericles* first performed. First printed 1609

1611 November 1 First Recorded production of *The Tempest*. First print 1623

1611-12 *Macbeth* First recorded performance. First printed 1623

1611-12 *Cymbeline* First recorded performance. First print 1623

1611-12 *The Winter's Tale* First recorded performance. First printed 1623

1612-13 *Henry VIII* first performance. First print 1623

1612-13 *The Two Noble Kinsmen*. First printed 1634